I0402537

Using Business Signs as an Effective Marketing Tool

A Step by Step Guide

By Meir Liraz

(Including 10 Special Bonuses)

Published by Liraz Publishing

www.BizMove.com

Copyright © Liraz Publishing. All rights reserved.

ISBN: 9781695674486

Table of Contents

1. Introduction

Have you considered the impact that your sign has on your business? This Guide discusses signs, what they can do for your business, and how they can be used to your advantage. A checklist for ordering a business sign is also provided.

Signs are one of the most efficient and effective means of communication. Signs help people find you; they reach people who are passing by your establishment; they present an image of your business. In short, signs, tell people who you are and what you are selling.

Signs are such a powerful communication medium that it is difficult to estimate the extent of their influence. Other media require the directed attention of the person receiving the message. Signs, however, can convey a message while creating a mood or feeling of atmosphere. It is not necessary for people to give full attention to your sign in order to derive meaning from its presence.

A sign is the most direct form of visual communication available. In fact, so many people use signs without a second thought that it is easy to overlook their importance. When we cannot talk to other people directly in a given location, we tack up signs: wet paint, beware of dog, enter here, garage sales, etc. signs are the only form of mass communication directly available to everyone - they are the people's street communication system.

2. What Signs Can Do for Your Business

Signs perform three major communications functions for your business; they give information and direction, provide a format for street advertising, and build your image.

Signs Give Information About Your Business and Direct People to Your Business Location.

Signs index the environment so people can find you. This is especially true for travelers, new members of your community, and impulse shoppers who may be on a journey to purchase a particular good or service which you sell. Americans are mobile. Each year 40 million of us travel over 1.7 trillion miles by automobile and approximately 19 per cent of us change our place of residence. A primary source of customers for your business is the large number of people who are new to your community or who may be just passing through. Your sign is the most effective way of reaching this mobile or transient group of potential customer.

Signs can correct a poor location by substituting effective communication for poor site characteristics. If your business is located on a site which is not visible or in a building which does not

not correspond with the goods or services offered, your sign can overcome this disability. For example, most buildings are not built to conform to the design needs of any particular type of tenant. Without an effective sign it is often impossible to determine what type of business is being conducted in a given building. In addition, when your site is located off a busy traffic artery or in an area which is not easily accessible your sign can communicate to people who are passing on a busy street several blocks away. If you are located off a busy freeway but far from an exit, your sign becomes your main device for directing people to your business. High-rise signs are used when a business is located away from potential customers' normal pathways of travel.

Signs Are Street Advertising

Your sign provides an easily recognizable display format for the goods or services you are selling. For most businesses the street is where potential customers are. The message conveyed on the street reaches people who are close enough to make a purchase.

Street advertising also help people develop a

memory of your business name and the products and services you sell. People tend to buy from businesses they know.

Signs can build an image for your business and help you identify with the market segment you are trying to reach.

Through materials and design, a sign can appeal to a given group of potential customers. For example, some firms attempt to capture the youth market,others senior citizens, others unmarried single people and so forth. If you have a particular market segment that you wish to attract to your business, your sign can be an important means of bringing these people in.

3. The Advantages of Signs

On-premise signs are your most effective and efficient means of commercial communication because they are inexpensive, available, practical, easy to use, always on the job, and directly oriented to the trade area of your business.

Signs Are Effective

Your sign is an integral part of your advertising program along with the other forms of commercial communication such as television, radio, newspapers, magazines, and billboards. There are four basic criteria used to judge the effectiveness of these advertising media: (1) coverage of the trade area, (2) repetition of a message, (3) readership of a message, and (4) cost per thousand exposures of a message. Two other criteria important for the small business owner are (5) availability and (6) ease of use. Let's see how signs measure to the above criteria.

1. Signs are oriented to your trade area. Signs do not waste your resources by requiring your to pay for wasted advertising coverage. The people who see your sign are the people who live in your trade area.

2. Signs are always on the job repeating your message to potential customers. Your on-premise sign communicates to potential customers twenty-four hours a day, seven days a week, week after week, month after month, year after year. Every time people pass your business establishment they see your sign. The mere repetition of the message will help them remember your business.

3. Nearly everyone reads signs. Signs are practical to use for nearly everyone is used to looking at signs and using signs, even small children. Studies have shown that people do read and remember what is on signs. When special items are displayed, sales increase for these particular items within the store.

4. Signs are inexpensive. When compared to the cost of advertising in some other media, the on-premise sign is very inexpensive. Table 1 indicates the cost-per-thousand-exposures for various media in a given type of community. Unless your trade area encompasses an entire city or region, where you must rely upon broad based media coverage, there is no better advertising dollar value than your on-premise sign.

5. Signs are available to each and every shop owner. There is no need to schedule the use of your sign. Your sign is available to you whenever you need it and to be used however you please.

6. Signs are easy to use. No special skills or resources are needed to operate a sign once it has been installed. If it is an illuminated sign, all you need to do is flip the switches and that may not be necessary with timing equipment. Once the initial expenditures are made no special resources or professional services are needed. You need only operate and maintain your sign.

4. Checklist for Ordering a Business Sign

Before you select a sign for your business there are several things you need to consider. A competent sign company in your area can help you with the answers to some of these question if you are unsure how to obtain them.

1. Who are your customers?

Potential customers for your business are people who reside in your trade area. Most of your customers come from the immediate area within a half mile to a mile of your business location. Trade areas come in assorted shapes and sizes depending upon the business. Trade areas may also vary seasonally.

2. How do you get information on potential customers?

Plot a dot map of your customers as soon as you begin business. This is easily done by plotting the addresses of people who stop in your store (and particularly of those who purchase) as a dot on a street map of your city. Within a few months time you will have a fairly clear idea of the trade area from which you are drawing your customers. You will then be able to decide what type of sign would best meet the needs of the people in that trade area. For example, if your customers can only reach you by automobile or you are located on a very busy street, the type of sign that you use will be very different than if you have a shopping center location and people must walk to your store from parking lots.

Obtain your street profile from a city traffic engineer. Since your sign communicates to people who pass your business establishment, you can direct your message to potential customers if you know what type of traffic passes your door. Your city traffic engineer can provide information which will tell you: where people begin and end their trips, how people travel, when people travel by time of day, why people travel, and where they park when they reach a destination. Even small cities and towns have traffic volume maps available to tell you how many people pass by your business every day.

Know how many new people move to your area each year. This is a potential market for your business. This type of information can be obtained from any board of realtors, chamber of commerce or police department.

3. How are you going to communicate with the customers?

In order to communicate effectively, a sign must be noticeable and readable.

A sign must be noticeable. After a while a sign becomes part of the landscape. It loses some of its ability to attract attention. By periodically changing some small design element or by using changeable copy, a sign can continue to attract interest. Time and temperature devices or rotating and moving parts can be used to maintain interest in a commercial message. Time and temperature devices or rotating and moving parts can be used to maintain interest in a commercial message. Time and temperature units also provide a needed public service.

A sign must be readable. A sign needs to be large enough to read. You need to know how far a person if from your store when he first sees your sign and the real speed of traffic on your street. With this information, a competent sign company can use a formula to calculate the necessary size for your design and build you an effective sign.

4. What are you trying to say?

Decide on a message that is clear and simple.

Focus on key words. Choose one or two words which describe your business. Clever or strange names may only attract certain customers.

Be Brief. The cleaner and clearer the message, the more impact it has. Listing or names or unclear symbols confuse rather than communicate.

5. What image are you trying to portray?

Design of your sign is very important. Your sign tells people a lot about your business. Stark simple design and materials may suggest discount prices and no frills. Elegant and expensive sign materials may suggest luxury goods and services. Two basic design considerations are important when ordering a sign.

Physical elements of sign design. These include considerations such as size, placement, materials and structure. The size of the sign is an important consideration for your business. The biggest sign that you can afford may not necessarily be the best one for your needs. A sign which is either too big or too small will not communicate your message effectively. The number of signs is also important. Too many signs compete with one another and reduce the effectiveness of your message by presenting an image of confusion to potential customers. The materials used for your sign determine its appearance and performance. For example, differences in cost, appearance, color, durability, flexibility and reaction to extreme weather conditions can be found in the many types of plastics available. The structure of a sign also contributes to its effectiveness. Pole covers and cantilevered construction help portray an attractive message. Figures 1 and 2 illustrate how physical elements of sign design affect business image.

Graphic elements of sign design. Graphic elements of design include layout of the message, colors, lettering, shape symbolism, harmony, and daytime versus nighttime lighting conditions.

Legibility is a test of good design. If your sign is well designed, it will be easy to read. Legibility means that the letters or characters on the sign are distinct from one another. Some color combinations of background and letters give excellent legibility while others are very poor. To test your sign's legibility, drive past your business and see if you can read it from a distance. Look at it both day and night. Some signs are difficult to read because of illumination problems such as glare from street lights, signs on nearby business establishments, or shadows caused by buildings. A well-designed sign blends with the environment, has a message impact and overcomes viewing problems.

6. How much should your sign cost?

You should consider several factors when determining the cost of your on-premise sign.

A sign is an investment. Your sign is one of the most permanent parts of your business and is exposed to weather and constant use. The average life of signs varies from five to eleven years, depending on type of materials used, construction and other factors. Find out how many years of service to expect from your sign. It pays to purchase good materials if you intend to use the sign over a period of years.

Maintenance costs. No business can afford to have its sign fall into disrepair. A dilapidated sign tells the public that you are not concerned with your business image or their visual environment. Some types of signs are virtually maintenance free while other require more attention. Find out how to replace burnt out bulbs or tubes in your sign. Determine who is responsible if the wind blows your sign down and someone is injured.

Energy consumption. New technological developments now enable some types of signs to achieve energy savings without sacrificing effects. Inquire about new energy saving bulbs and internal materials.

Owning or leasing. Many sign companies have programs whereby you can lease a sign for a given period of time and they will maintain it for you. This may be more economical for a new business, especially if there is any chance that logos or names may change in the first few years of operation. Statistics show that if a small business fails, it will happen somewhere between the first and second year of operation. Leasing a sign during this period of time might help save some of the initial capital needed for operating expenses.

Custom or standardized. Some large companies offer standardized types of signs which are cheaper than signs which are custom designed and constructed. Many of these standardized units can utilize ingenious design techniques to bring forth creativity and individuality. Often the standardized units can be arranged in different configurations depending on your needs. Some standardized sign units use the highest quality materials and are designed to be relatively maintenance free. Mass production enables these units to be sold much cheaper than if designed and produced from scratch.

7. Signs communicate in a shared environment.

A sign's ability to send its message beyond its locations requires that you be sensitive to the effects of your message on others. Since you share your space with others, consider their rights and sensibilities too. They are potential customers.

Consider city or town planning goals and regulation when ordering a sign. Some types of signs are not permitted. determine what the regulations are in your community before you discuss design with a sign designer. Most sign companies are well aware of the regulation in any given community and can guide you in selecting a sign which is not in violation of the law.

5. Understanding Your Customers

Small Business Customer Satisfaction Loyalty - understanding and achieving Customer Satisfaction Loyalty - is essential for commercial success. This guide explains how small companies can profit from understanding their customers.

Understanding one's customers is so important that large corporations spend hundreds of millions annually on market research. Although such formal research is important, a small firm can usually avoid this expense. Typically, the owner or manager of a small concern knows the customers personally. From this foundation, understanding of your customers can be built by a systematic effort. A comprehensive system for understanding is what Rudyard Kipling called his six honest serving men. "Their names are What and Why and When and How and Where and Who."

What Customer Satisfaction Loyalty

A seller characterizes what customers are buying as goods and services - toothpaste, drills, video games. cars. . . But understanding of buyers starts with the realization that they purchase benefits as well as products. Consumers don't select toothpaste.

Instead. some will pay for a decay preventive. Some seek pleasant taste. Others want bright teeth. Or perhaps any formula at a bargain price will do.

Similarly, industrial purchasing agents are not really interested in drills. They want holes. They insist on quality appropriate for their purposes, reliable delivery when needed, safe operation, and reasonable prices.

Video games are fun. They are bought for home entertainment, family togetherness, development of personal dexterity, introduction to computers, among other satisfactions. Commercial customers include arcades, pizza parlors, and assorted enterprises. They benefit from a potential source of income, a means of attracting buyers to their premises, or perhaps a competitive move.

Similarly, cars are visible evidence of a person's wealth, reflection of life style, a private cabin for romance. Or they represent receipts from leases, means to pursue an occupation. . . Some people even buy cars for transportation.

You must find out, from their point of view, what customers are buying. The common names of products mean as little to them as the chemical names on the label of a proprietary drug. (A sick person's real need is safe. speedy relief.) Understanding your customers enables you to profit by providing what buyers seeks - satisfaction.

Products change, but basic benefits like personal hygiene, attractiveness, safety, entertainment, and privacy endure. So do commercial purposes such as quests for competitive superiority or profitability.

Successful manufacturers and service establishments produce benefits for which customers are willing to pay. Successful wholesalers and retailers select offerings of such demanded benefits that they can resell at a profit. Successful businesspeople, in other words. understand the reason for their customers' buying decisions

Why Customer Relationship Management

The reason that customers buy is logical from their point of view. Understanding customers derives from this fundamental premise. Don't argue with taste.

Everybody is unique. Each person has individual pressures and criteria. Moreover, perceptions differ. The astute businessperson deduces and accepts the buying logic of customers and serves them accordingly.

To learn why customers buy can be quite difficult.

Some buyers hide their true motivations. In many cases the reasons are obscure to the buyers themselves. Most purchase decisions are multi-causal. Often, conflicts abound. A car buyer may want the roominess of a large vehicle and the fuel economy of a subcompact. The resolution of such mutually exclusive desires is usually indeterminate.

Sometimes the reasons why customers buy are trivial. If customers feel indifferent toward a product or store, the selection is apt to be happenstance. Perhaps several rival offerings meet all the conditions that a purchaser deems important. Consequently, minor factors govern. This explains the rationale of the consumer who chose a $ 22,000 car because its upholstery was most attractive. The point: Pay attention to details. They may be crucial to customers.

Often the best clues are the customers' actions. Shrewd businesspeople respect what people say, but pay special attention to what people do. More important than why customers buy is why former customers have taken their patronage elsewhere and why qualified buyers are not buying. What is now keeping them from buying?

Can this obstacle be surmounted? Businesspeople monitor competitive offerings and buyers' reactions to infer clues. Informal conversations may also reveal some reasons. Special offers may overcome resistance and boost profits.

All the time the manager must be careful to retain the company's regular customers. For instance, a specialty dress shop may try to widen its patronage through a new line at bargain prices. This move could disturb the store's usual patrons. They may take their trade to another store that caters exclusively to their social class.

Many of the dresses were bought for special occasions when projection of a genteel image was important to the customer. Understanding of customers includes awareness of the time of the purchase and use of the merchandise.

When

A seller must be ready when the buyer is, lest an

opportunity be irretrievably lost. Customers buy when they want an offering and have the time and money to purchase it. Buying patterns can often be discerned from an analysis of customers and their purchases. For example, wants for many consumer goods and services are tied to customers' rites of passage. The following purchase occasions in the adult life cycle are typical:

1. Marriage, separation, divorce

2. Acquisition of a home

3. Change in employment or career

4. Graduate study; running for office

5. Health care, injury, illness

6. Pregnancy, nurture of children

7. Children enter school; graduate

8. Children leave home (for college or permanently)

9. Move to another area

10. Vacations; major social activities

11. Permanent retirement from work

12. Death of a family member.

Shrewd retailers keep track of such key buying events and gain a head start on making sales. Logs of birthdays and anniversaries are a case in point. Additional purchase occasions are impersonal. Seasonal factors include recurring holidays and weather changes. Among other favorable influences on purchases are start of the school year, semi-annual white sales, introduction of new models and clearance of old ones, special price concessions, and improvement in economic conditions or buyer's confidence.

Some of the latter factors also apply to manufacturers. Small plants work closely with their buyers' inventory managers and replenish stock at their reorder point. A current vogue is just-in-time delivery. Interactive computers make replenishment notices routine.

Many consumers have time for shopping only during off-hours. in the evenings, and on weekends. The trend from a single breadwinner per family toward having all adults of a household engage in commercial employment has intensified this time peculiarity. Astute retailers adjust their hours, staffing, and availability of merchandise to customers' shopping convenience. Bartenders know that business booms on payday. Manufacturers profit from timing their offers to their customers' budgetary cycles. Thus, knowing when products are bought and used is a valuable facet of understanding customers.

Although a transaction may be concluded in a moment, most purchases actually entail a drawn-out process.

This process will be described in the next section which analyzes how customers buy.

How

Knowledge of how customers buy pays off in several ways. (1) Sellers can design their offerings to meet the exact needs of their buyers. (2) Sellers can influence decision makers at crucial steps of the buying process. (3) Sellers can lay the groundwork for repeat business.

Buying methods are best visualized as processes. Household purchases usually start when a consumer has a desire or a problem that an acquisition might satisfy or solve. Industrial purchases usually start when a user or a routine sets off a signal (requisition) for approval of a procurement.

People are diverse. Every consumer, every firm pursues a buying process of its own. Buying processes also depend on the significance of the product to the buyer and on other circumstances. Although buying processes are not uniform. some steps are common to most of them. The seller needs to know only these critical steps when he or she can affect the outcome of the buying decision.

Shrewd sellers delve into the behavioral milestones of purchasers. But for each very important customer the buying process should be diagrammed individually, showing names of influencers at each decision stage, elapsed time between stages, and any other pertinent information.

Perhaps a change in life style or a demonstration at a friend's house has caused this consumer to recognize the need for a personal computer. But lack of knowledge and the fear of a wrong decision may counteract this desire. The process continues, however, if advertisements and expected benefits persuade the consumer to act. Despite budgetary constraints and uncertainty about future needs, the consumer proceeds to compare stores and brands.

At this search and evaluation stage advice from

present satisfied customers is especially influential. Make sure your customers are satisfied and favorably recommend your merchandise or service. To the contrary, poor shopping facilities or irritating personnel can sway the potential customer against making the purchase from you.

Sooner or later, further search does not seem worthwhile. If the positives still outweigh the negatives, the consumer picks a store and brand. The transaction itself is consummated quickly, assuming the wanted item is available. The satisfied customer makes recommendations to others and gives you his or her repeated, regular business.

Businesspeople can create sales by predisposing potential buyers to their product or store. Manufacturers can offer exclusive benefits in their goods, such as friendly relations, efficient operations, and easy manuals. Enticing advertisements help persuade prospects to visit a retail outlet and ask about a particular brand. Creative salespeople overcome the customer's objections and doubts and close the sale. Post-transaction service keeps the customer satisfied. Referrals usually follow.

Specific details are needed to track acquisition of something complex, say a computer. On the other hand, less detail is needed if the purchase is laundry detergent or some other staple with which the customer is less involved. In the latter case, depletion of the home inventory triggers a routine, leading directly to choice: the usually purchased brand. If the usual brand is out-of-stock or another brand is on sale. a substitute may be bought quickly. Brand comparisons follow or may be omitted.

Some products are bought when an emergency need for them arises. A physical examination and the filling of a prescription are urgent when sickness strikes. Arrangements for funerals follow immediately after the death of a family member. Umbrellas are in demand when it rains. An unexpected snow storm generates extra calls for tire chains, towing services, and car batteries. Often, convenient availability determines when these goods and services are purchased. And even if customers do have ample time to select merchandise, sellers who stand ready to supply wanted or expected brands are apt to gain preference and profit when shoppers decide where to buy.

People want options. Although convenient availability is the main buying criterion for many routine household products, savvy merchants stock a selection conforming to the diverse preferences of their patrons. Some people demand manufacturers' advertised brands. Resellers' brands are favored by others. On some classes of goods, generic brands have become popular in recent years. Moreover, many consumers seek occasional variety. Clearly the decision of which products to stock is important.

It is more important yet on shopping goods because buyers compare them before purchase. And it is most important on specialty goods, those preselected by brand name. If a store does not stock these uniquely wanted brands, a prospect will leave without buying. Whoever offers them on acceptable terms gains the sale.

Where Business Customer Relationship Management

From a multitude of studies emerge different criteria for deciding where to shop. Most research on the subject agrees that store location is a major consideration, Stores usually draw most of their patronage from their surrounding neighborhood.

Savvy store managers make a special effort to understand the shopping-related motivations and preferences of local residents. New managers of fast-food units, for example, canvass nearby dwellings and introduce themselves to the households. Some supermarkets maintain consumer advisory boards to elicit suggestions and reactions. Other means of communication with customers include informal conversations at the store and suggestion boxes with interviews and awards.

Incidentally, complaints are an excellent guide for making store policies more amenable to customers. Personnel should be instructed to thank patrons for their comments. Prompt consideration, followed by a personal letter from the store manager, is highly desirable.

Location is extremely important to "captive" buyers. Exclusively franchised utilities, shops in isolated hotels. and cafeterias or automatic vending machines in factories are examples. At the opposite extreme, shoppers escape spatial restrictions by buying from mail-order firms or telephone solicitors.

Other patronage influences vary. They depend on

the type of product. type of store, and the characteristics of the consumer. The offered assortment's perceived quality. depth, and breadth certainly are very important. along with price, This does not imply that all goods have to be top quality or all prices the lowest. Perceptions are decisive.

If quality seems high, some customers infer that prices are high too regardless of the facts. The important point is to understand customers and to provide what causes them to buy. For example, assurance of repair service weighs heavily with the worrier type of customer. A convenience-minded buyer is concerned with parking space or delivery service.

Of course, shoppers must be told that wanted goods and services are available. Advertising helps disseminate this information. So does a store's reputation for consistent policies of satisfying its customers.

Occasional promotions inject some excitement into the tedium of shopping. Some clients like to socialize, which can absorb much of an employee's time and may even annoy other buyers. Nevertheless, personnel should be friendly and helpful. Also influential, for some customers, is the apparent socio-economic level of other shoppers.

Personal affinity for other customers or for salespeople is a decisive factor in the success of party-selling, e.g., household goods and in-home selling (cosmetics). The choice of where to buy items requiring major outlays (securities, and insurance) often revolves around from whom to buy.

In selecting a retail store, many customers consider physical features. Layouts can invite or repel patronage. Motorists who are in a hurry, for instance, are apt to use a gasoline station at which business can be transacted quickly. Altogether, buyers perceive a mix of tangible and intangible factors that comprise a store's atmosphere. Accordingly, they either do or don't feel comfortable about shopping there.

To the casual observer, all supermarkets seem more or Hess alike, But. in fact, store managers can regulate many of the above-mentioned variables and thereby affect where shoppers buy. According to recent studies in several American cities, household buyers perceive supermarkets in their neighborhood as sufficiently different to determine their patronage preference. The four main types of supermarkets offer: (1) High quality at commensurate prices, (2) Lowest price level in the area, (3) Swift completion, (4) Friendly atmosphere. Each can profit by appealing to a different segment of buyers. the topic of the next section.

Who

Identification of customers and prospects makes effective targeting possible. Small business owners pride themselves on knowing their customers personally. In the industrial field, understanding of each major customer and buying influence is essential. When dealing with a large number of customers, however, individual familiarity is not feasible. Hence mass merchandisers and others in this situation group their customers, whose reactions to offerings are similar, into segments. Then they design a separate appropriate marketing program for each segment.

Strategies vary, A small firm might prosper by concentrating its resources on one segment. Because customers are volatile, the specializing firm is vulnerable to sudden change in its target segment's patronage. Hence some companies address several segments simultaneously. Although expensive, a strategy of employing different tactics for different segments can be quite profitable. Other firms scatter offers to just anybody. They hope that segments will select themselves.

One basis for segmentation is geographic. Retail customers are apt to live or work in the store's vicinity. Industrial buyers tend to concentrate regionally. So do users of services. Intensive cultivation of local potential customers can be efficient and lucrative. Personal knowledge of local buyers and a shared community spirit help cement relations with these customers.

Segmentation is an art. All "honest serving men" - what, why, when, how, where, as well as who - can be the key to segmentation. Whatever the basis, each identified segment should have sufficient purchasing power to make a special effort commercially worthwhile. Accessibility is vital. How can the segment be reached? Are advertisements, telephone solicitations, or personal visits efficient? How about trade shows or personal contacts? The ideal segment is stable in purchase needs and loyalty, helping you fend off competition.

Besides segmentation, understanding of customers also requires insight into their buying roles. The buyer for a one-person household or one-person business is the initiator of the order, the decider, and the user. Even in this case, however, some outsiders are influential.

In larger households or businesses, these buying roles are usually played by separate individuals. It helps you to know who activates (requisitions) purchases, who exerts influence, who decides what and where to buy, who uses the product-and what their criteria are. Then you tailor and target your offerings to satisfy each major participant in the buying process.

As has been shown, understanding of customers enables a seller to increase sales. This same understanding can equally serve to reduce costs. Higher sales at lower costs inevitably boost profits.

A small firm that understands its customers can buy or produce exactly what they want-and nothing else. The firm's sales effort is efficient because it builds on why its customers want to buy not on why others buy, or why the vendor wants to sell.

Merchandise can be ready when customers need it.

Thus a knowledgeable seller avoids unnecessary inventory costs or penalties for late delivery. Understanding how customers buy lets a seller employ promotional media, appeals, and timing for maximum effectiveness. Transportation costs are lowered by shipping merchandise to where it is needed. Knowledge of who comprises suitable segments and the separate buying roles can reduce the waste of soliciting unqualified or uninterested people.

Customers Are Dynamic - Customer Satisfaction Loyalty

The best source for you to learn about customers is your personal interaction with them. At work, social and civic activities, and chance encounters, people talk and reveal their attitudes and motivation. Listen to your customers. You can also keep abreast of purchasing patterns by observing competitors' practices and by asking sales personnel who is buying what, where.

Articles in business and trade newspapers and magazines give information on products, trends, marketing, finance, the economy. Trade directories, Yellow Pages, and brokers' direct-mail lists identify who buyers are, and most industries have associations and specialized marketing research that provide insights for understanding customers.

6. How to Make the Right Decisions

Everyone is a decision maker. We all rely on information, and techniques or tools, to help us in our daily lives. When we go out to eat, the restaurant menu is the tool that provides us with the information needed to decide what to purchase and how much to spend. Operating a business also requires making decisions using information and techniques - how much inventory to maintain, what price to sell it at, what credit arrangements to offer, how many people to hire.

Decision making in business is the systematic process of identifying and solving problems, of asking questions and finding answers. Decisions usually are made under conditions of uncertainty. The future is not known and sometimes even the past is suspect. This guide opens the door for business owners and managers to learn about the variety of techniques which can be used to improve decision making in a world of uncertainty, change, and uncontrollable circumstances.

A General Approach to Decision Making

Whether a scientist, an executive of a major corporation, or a small business owner, the general approach to systematically solving problems is the same. The following 7 step approach to better management decision making can be used to study nearly all problems faced by a business.

1. State the problem

A problem first must exist and be recognized. What is the problem and why is it a problem. What is ideal and how do current operations vary from that ideal. Identify why the symptoms (what is going wrong) and the causes (why is it going wrong). Try to define all terms, concepts, variables, and relationships. Quantify the problem to the extent possible. If the problem, not accurately and quickly filling customer orders, try to determine how many orders were incorrectly filled and how long it took to fill them.

2. Define the Objectives

What are the objectives of the study. Which objectives are the most critical. Objectives usually are stated by an action verb like to reduce, to increase, or to improve. Returning to the customer order problem, the major objectives would be: 1) to increase the percentage of orders filled correctly, and 2) to reduce the time it takes to process and order. A subobjective could include to simplify and streamline the order filling process.

3. Develop a Diagnostic Framework

Next establish a diagnostic framework, that is, decide what methods are going to be used, what kinds of information are needed, and how and where the information is to be found. Is there going to be a customer survey, a review of company documents, time and motion tests, or something else. What are the assumptions (facts assumed to be correct) of the study. What are the criteria used to judge the study. What time, budget, or other constraints are there. What kind of quantitative or other specific techniques are going to be used to analyze the data. (Some of which will be covered shortly). In other words, the diagnostic framework establishes the scope and methods of the entire study.

4. Collect and Analyze the Data

The next step is to collect the data (by following the methods established in Step 3. Raw data is then tabulated and organized to facilitate analysis. Tables, charts, graphs, indexes and matrices are some of the standard ways to organize raw data. Analysis is the critical prerequisite of sound business decision making. What does the data reveal. What facts, patterns, and trends can be seen in the data. Many of the quantitative techniques covered below can be used during the step to determine facts, patterns, and trends in data. Of course, computers are used extensively during this step.

5. Generate Alternative Solutions

After the analysis has been finished, some specific conclusions about the nature of the problem and its resolution should have been reached. The next step is to develop alternative solutions to the problem and rank them in order of their net benefits. But how are alternatives best generated. Again, there are several well established techniques such as the Nominal Group Method, the Delphi Method and Brainstorming, among others. In all these methods a group is involved, all of whom have reviewed the data and analysis. The approach is to have an informed group suggesting a variety of possible solutions.

6. Develop an Action Plan and Implement

Select the best solution to the problem but be certain to understand clearly why it is best, that is, how it achieves the objectives established in Step 2 better than its alternatives. Then develop an effective method (Action Plan) to implement the solution. At this point an important organizational consideration arises - who is going to be responsible for seeing the implementation through and what authority does he have. The selected manager should be responsible for seeing that all tasks, deadlines, and reports are performed, met, and written. Details are important in this step: schedules, reports, tasks, and communication are the key elements of any action plan. There are several techniques available to decision makers implementing an action plan. The PERT method is a way of laying out an entire period such as an action plan. PERT will be covered shortly.

7. Evaluate, obtain Feedback and Monitor

After the Action Plan has been implemented to solve a problem, management must evaluate its effectiveness. Evaluation standards must be determined, feedback channels developed, and monitoring performed. This Step should be done after 3 to 5 weeks and again at 6 months. The goal is to answer the bottom line question. Has the problem been solved?

7. Improving Your Delegation Skills

Derived from Latin, delegate means "to send from."
When delegating you are sending the work "from"
you "to" someone else. Effective delegation Skills
will not only give you more time to work on your
important opportunities, but you will also help
others on your team learn new skills.

Here are some tips that will help you improve your
delegation skills - delegation of work.

- Delegation helps people grow underneath you in
  an organization and thus pushes you even higher
  in management. It provides you with more time,
  and you will be able to take on higher priority
  projects.

- Delegate whole pieces or entire job pieces rather
  than simply tasks and activities.

- Clearly define what outcome is needed, then let
  individuals use some creative thinking of their
  own as to how to get to that outcome.

- Clearly define limits of authority that go with the
  delegated job. Can the person hire other people
  to work with them? Are there spending
  constraints?

- Clear standards of performance will help the person know when he or she is doing exactly what is expected.

- When on the receiving end of delegation, work to make your boss' job easier and to get the boss promoted. This will enhance your promotability also.

- Assess routine activities in which you are involved. Can any of them be eliminated or delegated?

- Never underestimate a person's potential. Delegate slightly more than you think the person is capable of handling. Expect them to succeed, and you will be pleasantly surprised more frequently than not.

- Expect completed staff work from the individuals reporting to you. That is, they will come to you giving you alternatives and suggestions when a problem exists rather than just saying "Boss, what should we do?"

- Do not avoid delegating something because you cannot give someone the entire project. Let the person start with a bite size piece, then after learning and doing that, they can accept larger pieces and larger areas of responsibility.

- Agree on a monitoring or measurement procedure that will keep you informed as to progress on this project because you are ultimately still responsible for it and need to know that it is progressing as it should. In other words-If you can't measure it don't delegate it.

- Keep your mind open to new ideas and ways of doing things. There just might be a better way than the way something has previously been done.

- Delegation is not giving an assignment. You are asking the person to accept responsibility for a project. They have the right to say no.

- Encourage your people to ask for parts of your job.

- Never take back a delegated item because you can do it better or faster. Help the other person learn to do it better.

- Agree on the frequency of feedback meetings or reports between yourself and the person to whom you are delegating. Good communication will assure ongoing success.

- Delegation strengthens your position. It shows you are doing your job as a manager-getting results with others. This makes you more promotable.

- Delegation is taking a risk that the other person might make a mistake, but people learn from mistakes and will be able to do it right the next time. Think back to a time a project was delegated to you and you messed it up. You also learned a valuable lesson.

- Find out what the talents and interests of your people are and you will be able to delegate more intelligently and effectively.

- A person will be more excited about doing a project when they came up with the idea of how to do it, than if the boss tells them how to do it.

- Be sensitive to upward delegation by your staff. When they ask you for a decision on their project, ask them to think about some alternatives which you will then discuss with them. This way responsibility for action stays with the staff member.

- Don't do an activity that someone else would be willing to do for you if you would just ask them.

- "Push" responsibility down in a caring helpful way.

- Remember, you are not the only one that can accomplish an end result. Trust others to be capable of achieving it.

- Break large jobs into manageable pieces and delegate pieces to those who can do them more readily.

- Keep following up and following through until the entire project is done. Break large jobs into manageable pieces and delegate pieces to those who can do them more readily.

- Resist the urge to solve someone else's problem. They need to learn for themselves. Give them suggestions and perhaps limits but let them take their own action.

Appendix: Special Free Bonuses

You can access your free bonuses here:

https://www.bizmove.com/bizgifts.htm

Here's what you get:

#1 How to Be a Good Manager and Leader; 120 Tips to improve your Leadership Skills (Leadership Video Guide).

Learn how to improve your leadership skills and become a better manager and leader. Here's how to be the boss people want to give 200 percent for. In this video you'll discover 120 powerful tips and strategies to motivate and inspire your people to bring out the best in them.

#2 Small Business Management: Essential Ingredients for Success (eBook Guide)

Discover scores of business management tricks, secrets and shortcuts. This Ebook guide does far more than impart knowledge - it inspires action.

#3 How to Manage Yourself for Success; 90 Tips to Better Manage Yourself and Your Time (Self Management Video Guide)

You are responsible for everything that happens in your life. Learn to accept total responsibility for yourself. If you don't manage yourself, then you are letting others have control of your life. In this video you'll discover 90 powerful tips and strategies to better manage yourself for success.

#4 80 Best Inspirational Quotes for Success (Motivational Video Guide)

For this video we scanned thousands of motivational and inspirational quotes to bring you this collection of the best 80 motivational quotes for success in life.

#5 Top 10 Habits to Adopt From Highly Successful People (Self Growth Video Guide)

In this video you'll discover the top 10 habits of highly successful people that you can adopt and achieve success in your life.

#6 Personal Branding: How to Make a Killer First Impression (Self Promotion Video Guide)

This video deals with personal branding. While promoting your personal brand, you'll discover in this video the ten most effective things you can do to make the best first impression possible.

#7 How to Advance Your Career 10 Times Faster (Career Advancement Video Guide)

The most important thing to remember about your

career today is that you need to be responsible for your own future. In this video you'll discover 10 powerful strategies to advance your career faster.

#8 How to Get Success in Life; 10 Strategies to Attract the Life You Want (Self Actualization Video Guide)

To have more, we must be more of who we are. The secret is in the doing; none of it matters until we do something about it. In this video you'll discover 10 powerful strategies to attract the life you want.

#9 A Comprehensive Package of Business Tools

Here's a collection featuring dozens of business related templates, worksheets, forms, and plans; covering finance, starting a business, marketing, business planning, sales, and general management.

#10 People Management Skills: How to Deal with Difficult Employees (Managing People Video Guide)

Problem behavior on the part of employees can erupt for a variety of reasons. In this video you'll discover the top ten ideas for dealing with difficult employees.

www.ingramcontent.com/pod-product-compliance
Lightning Source LLC
Chambersburg PA
CBHW070837220526
45466CB00002B/809

* 9 7 8 1 6 9 5 6 7 4 4 8 6 *